Mel Bay's
FUN WITH THE PAN FLUTE
R E V I S E D E D I T I O N

by Kristopher Faubion

CD Contents

1 Exercise One [1:00]	32 Harvest Home [:55]	62 Exercise Nine [:52]
2 Exercise Two [:57]	33 Scherzo [:15]	63 Exercise Ten [:36]
3 The First Nowell [:54]	34 Polovetsian Dances [:46]	64 Pentatunic [2:02]
4 Now All the Woods Are Sleeping [:50]	35 Mãruntel [:39]	65 Exercise Eleven [:40]
5 Ode to Joy [:38]	36 Wayfaring Stranger [:47]	66 Angels We Have Heard On High [:50]
6 Morning [:35]	37 Baidin Fheidhilmid [1:09]	67 Aura Lee [1:00]
7 Joy to the World [:36]	38 Come, Ever Smiling Liberty [:57]	68 We Three Kings of Orient Are [:44]
8 Joy of Friendship [:55]	39 Exercise Six [:48]	69 Nelly Bly [:49]
9 Exercise Three [1:18]	40 Jingle Bells [:45]	70 Pied Piper [:34]
10 Kum Ba Ya [:48]	41 My Bonnie [:46]	71 'Tis the Last Rose of Summer [:55]
11 Humming Song [:37]	42 O Come, All Ye Faithful [1:09]	72 Yellow Rose of Texas [:30]
12 All Through the Night [1:25]	43 Hush Little Baby [:18]	73 March of the Toys [:33]
13 Gary Owen [:36]	44 Wildwood Flower [:32]	74 Exercise Twelve [:29]
14 The Jasmine Flower [:42]	45 Two Little Sisters [:55]	75 Streets of Laredo [:32]
15 Swing Low, Sweet Chariot [:54]	46 Song of the Lark [:38]	76 Deck the Hall [:32]
16 Kimigayo [:41]	47 Kingdom Coming [:46]	77 Hark! The Herald Angels Sing [:59]
17 Theme from "Surprise Symphony" [1:28]	48 Exercise Seven [:34]	78 March [:46]
18 The Farmer and the Crow [:19]	49 Silent Night [1:03]	79 Gigue [1:03]
19 Exercise Four [:54]	50 Jesu, Joy of Man's Desiring [1:23]	80 O Katy O'Neil [1:06]
20 Down in the Valley [:26]	51 Theme from Fantasia I [:56]	81 Theme-Sonata [:46]
21 Ye Banks & Braes [:37]	52 The Happy Farmer [:48]	82 Senka Tankana [1:13]
22 Shenandoah [:46]	53 Country Dance [:41]	83 The Miller's Flowers [:42]
23 Riddle Song [:34]	54 Exercise Eight [:53]	84 Las Mañanitas [:37]
24 The Merry Plowboy [:33]	55 Melody [1:16]	85 The Little Sandman's Song [:44]
25 Paddy Whack [:43]	56 Minuet [:43]	86 Symphony No. 1 [:41]
26 A-Roving [:36]	57 Sonatina [:31]	87 Carolan's Receipt [1:05]
27 Serenade [:41]	58 The Idle Road [:50]	88 Mazurka [:17]
28 Simple Gifts [:45]	59 Hatikvah [:44]	89 Love is Teasin' [1:03]
29 God Rest You Merry, Gentlemen [:39]	60 Annie Laurie [:40]	90 Shule Aroon [:42]
30 Exercise Five [:50]	61 Songs My Mother Taught Me [1:00]	91 The Ould Orange Flute [1:00]
31 O Christmas Tree! [:39]		

1 2 3 4 5 6 7 8 9 0

Visit us on the Web at www.melbay.com — E-mail us at email@melbay.com

Table of Contents

Preface

With this book and CD you can learn to play the panpipe. That includes learning to 'read music.' and *semi-tone bending, with* the method, exercises, and tunes in this book. Some "prelude:"

◊   The tunes and exercises need a *panpipe* with the range of fifteen pipes starting at the G' above middle C'

◊   All the tunes and exercises listed in the table of contents are found on the CD.

◊   An index on the last page will help you locate a tune quickly, and 'track numbers' by each tune

◊   The *tempo marks* in the book and the tempos on the CD are merely suggested rates.

◊   *Dynamic contrasts* are notated in some songs throughout the book, but not always in the same tunes on the CD. 'Contrasts are an advanced technique for 'wind instruments' with each `wind type` needing a special technique for." You'll find the pan flute technique for `contrasts in this book. Play the tunes at a tempo that pleases you, with or without the `contrasts. Each soloist (that's you) can be the music *arranger / conductor.*

◊   Many of the tunes have *repeats* that would not fit on the full CD. The repeats are not included in the book notation either. *Double bar lines (for song verses)* may imply a repeat that is "missing'. You may freely repeat a measure, a phrase, a staff, or an entire tune.

About the Instrument

Pan flute is another name for the panpipe due in part to the tone color that the panpipe shares with flutes. The closer similarity is that you play both the flute and panpipe with the same lip position and shape known as *embouchure.* Technically, the pan flute is a scale row of whistle-flutes. Nevertheless, throughout this book, you will see both names for the instrument to promote the relative accuracy of both names. A more accurate name might well be the "panpipe-flute" or the "pan-flute pipes." "Pan-tubes" is 'science lingo' and even more accurate than 'panpipe.' Furthermore, for the sake of fun, we disregard the nagging 'syntax questions': "two words 'pan flute' or one word 'panpipe'," and "to hyphenate or not to hyphenate"...

Each panpipe pipe has a closed end known as the *foot* and open 'playing end' known as the *mouth*. By contrast, the flute foot is open and its mouth end is closed. That difference creates a tone color (*timbre*) difference between the panpipe and the flute. Compare the panpipe tone with the flute, recorder, and pipe organ. Which one sounds closest to the panpipe? (A pipe organ with all its pipes made of bamboo "lives playing" in the Philippines.) Re pan and flutes:

◊   It is most often made of reed or wood rather than metal from which most organ pipes are made

◊   As the earliest pipe organ, the *panpipe* uses the player's breath as the organ bellows.

◊   *Pan*, in addition to the name of the 'Greek inventor of the panpipe,' means "many."

◊   A panpipe has many (pan) *wind chambers* (pipes) that make a useful range of tones.

◊   A flute has one wind chamber with finger-holes that change the length of the pipe, creating its range of tones.

◊   You can find the panpipe in the music on all six (inhabitable) continents and many islands.

◊   It is manifest in the music of the Andes mountain region. The native Qheswa play a variety of voiced panpipes rhythmically, melodically, and harmonically in ensemble playing. The Qheswan groups perform and record their abundant traditional and original music.

◊   Romanians pan flutists, notably Zamphir and Syrinx, brought worldwide attention to the panpipe as a solo instrument. With "serious music" orchestral accompaniment, they perform an array of music styles on the pan flute. Some of the compositions they perform, unlike most music for the pan flute, modulate from one key to another. To accomplish this, they bend tones to play *semi-tones.*

The allure of the pan flute, for both musician and listener, is more than its antiquity:

•   A well-proportioned pan flute gives a quick, loud low tones in contrast to the recorder and flute.

•   In contrast to the other 'flute-winds', a well-designed panpipe decreases in 'decibel loudness' with each higher pipe (because of the graduated diameters of each pipe).

•   The pan flute tone color perks our ears with a nuance of other tones that we know such as an ice-cream organ and a riverboat calliope. Some think they hear the panpipe as a 'haunting or scary tone.' The tune, playing style, type of pan flute, and *studio effects* will, of course, effect the emotion evoked in the audience. Beyond that, what do you hear, is it important that you hear it, and like or dislike it?

Kristopher Faubion,
January 26, 2003

How to Play the Pan Flute

About the instrument: **The pipes are 'graduated' so that** each shorter pipe is narrower than the previous longer. **The open ends (*mouths*) have a 'flat, smooth, edge' (*playing surface*) that you place to your lips. "*Which side do you play?*" Place the concave, 'inner curve' of the pipes to your lips.**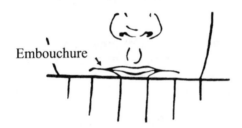

◊ Hold the 'pipes with both hands: your **right** hand around the bases (*feet*) or between the *support braces* of the longest two pipes, and your **left** hand propping the short end pipes as seen in Figure 2.

◊ *Embouchure:* stretch lips into a thin, flat, and firm 'half-smile.' For the best playing results, keep them consistently stretched thin, flat, and firm so that you may easily move the pipes laterally making melody.

◊ Part your lips just enough so that you can blow the breath stream the goes over one pipe exclusive of the others. You will need to narrow your breath stream a bit for each narrower pipe.

◊ Bring the pipes to your embouchure, with the longest pipe to your **right**. – Place the playing surface at the middle of your lower lip. Use a mirror to see that the pipes are placed on your lip on the bottom half of your lip. Center the pipe that you will play on your embouchure so that you can '*aim your thin stream of breath*' over it exclusive of the other pipes (that gets a bit 'trickier' with each narrower pipe).

◊ Blow with force from your diaphragm to get the quick, clear tone especially for the long / low pipes. Pronounce the letter 'T to give your breath an 'extra burst'

◊ Blow across the pipe mouth to get the tone truest to the pitch. (Blowing into the pipe will 'flatten' pitch, and will help to bend semi-tones lower, which is an advance technique.)

◊ Move the pipes to the next pipe you want play. Keep your head still, and at a consistent angle.

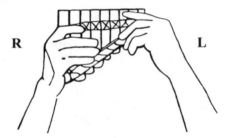

To 'move the pipes laterally':
1. Release the pressure of the 'played pipe' on your embouchure
2. Bring the 'pipes slightly away from
3. Move the set over to the next pipe to be played
4. Bring the 'pipes back onto your embouchure re-applying pressure the 'short distance intervals'

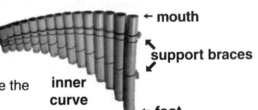

To 'move the pipes a short distance':
◊ Release the pressure as before, but keep the playing surface on your embouchure.
◊ Slide from the pipe you played to the next one to be played.
◊ Maintain your embouchure, stop blowing as you slide the playing surface across your embouchure. (Keep blowing for the *glissando* or *flourish* effect , what you hear when you run the back of your hand over several piano keys).
◊ Reduce friction by applying food oil / grease onto the playing surface. Moisture in constant supply from your mouth will do the same. Moisture condenses from your breath into and around the pipe mouths to enhance tone as you play. Your moist lips will give you more control over your breath and tone quality.

Interval: The Distance Between Pipes

The skill of pan flute playing is to accurately moving from the pipe you played to the next pipe you want to play. You, without being able to see it, you sense that interval. (It takes a similar skill, and a more fully "trained ear" to play the trombone and violin. It takes that skill to play piano or guitar whist reading music on the page.) Practice the following eight 'Fun With Exercises' well enough to play each interval without looking at the notation. Then

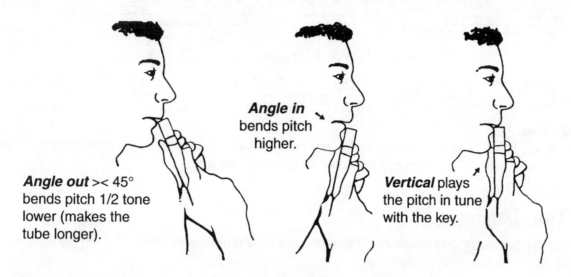

Angle out >< 45° bends pitch 1/2 tone lower (makes the tube longer).

Angle in bends pitch higher.

Vertical plays the pitch in tune with the key.

Care for the Pan Flute

Lube the inside walls to enhance tone, and protect: with any light oil " ◆ monthly if you play often, or live in the 'rain forest' ◆ with either tube brush, percolator brush, or plumber's pipe brush, "◆ with two 'tube size' brushes for the wider pipe diameters (greater than `$E^2$`) ◆ or with a flute swab with soft cloth laced onto it" or with a kid's and adult's size medium bristle toothbrush" ◆ a "light lube" with oil on a toothbrush over the pipe mouths protects the most exposed area" ◆ make the playing surface smooth with ultra-fine sandpaper or a terry-cloth, or clean leather Clean the outside walls: ◆ with mild soapy warm water or any 'mist cleanser,' and a soft brush or cloth" with soft cloth f or towel-off with soft cloth for towel-off

Prevent these:
"Dance on" pan flute • "Dog on" panpipe • Storm damage • "Pan-pipe / door-jamming" • Sun-burn.

About the Author

• Fully evolved member of the *Homo sapiens* (no horns, tail, or hooves).
• Self-taught (with books) flutist including the pan flute, he played the flute for a while in a community orchestra, 'sat-in' with a Baroque ensemble playing, on the pan flute, the majestic *"Senka Tankana"*, which you will find on page 36,
• Likes to play spontaneously when the "spirit moves," and is certain that though natural 'song and dance' may not 'save the day' it does make life more meaningful.
• Prefers audiences of birds and landscapes for several reasons, not the least of which is "they care not about a wrong note because they'll not miss a beat."
• Plays the guitar as he pleases, and sings in choirs when he can.
• Aspires to, one day, get a tone via blowing between the 'creases of his thumbs with hands cupped together,' and to make more merry mirth.
www.pan-pipes.com

Exercise One: *Crawling*

Play the 'F pipe (in the middle of the pipes) until you make good tone quickly. Play `F along with neighbors `E and `G until you play the trio with quick, clear, and steady tone. Add another until you can play all with ease.

 track 1

Toddling...

Articulation:

Pronounce the letter 'T' to give each tone its "own space" between the next and previous tone. Pronounce the letters 'P', 'K', and the syllable 'huh' for fun and effects.

Exercise Two: *Walking*

Play each pipe to hear *major and minor 2nd intervals. Pick up the tempo* as the quality of your tone and accuracy improves.

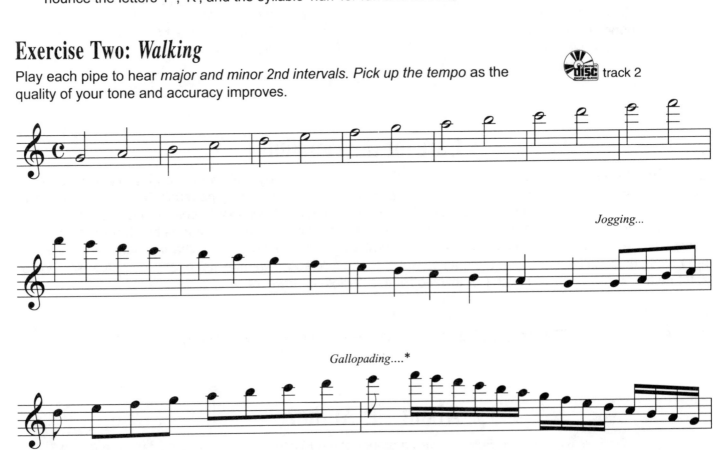

Jogging...

Gallopading....*

Make quick tone: focus and aim your breath so that all of it goes over one mouth only. Narrow your breath stream for each smaller mouth by closing your lips.

Stretch your lips out as if to smile. Bring your jaw back a bit. Part your lips slightly at the middle so that you blow a thin stream aimed across one mouth.

Moisture, moisture, 'moist your lips helps you to control your breath stream, and improve tone quality.

* A *Galop* is a very lively, spirited *round dance* in 2/4 time derived from the old German *Hopse* or *Ruttsher* (names descriptive of the steps), and introduced in France in the 19th century.

The First Nowell

track 3

England

A *tie* line *joins two tones <u>of the same pitch</u> as one continuous tone without articulation (pause of silence) between the tones.* • Tied notes are present in songs with lyrics hyphenated into one syllable per note. • Tied notes over a *bar line* removes the 'first note accent' from that next measure. See *slurs* page 36.

track 4

Now All The Woods Are Sleeping

J.S. Bach
1685-1750

A *comma* **,** between two notes warns, "Pause for breath (lest ye hyperventilate) and or dramatic effect without changing the time value of the notes in the measure."

track 5

Ode To Joy

Beethoven 1770-1827

< Crescendo: gradually louder `*f*` > Decrescendo: gradually quieter `*p*`

:|| ← *Repeat:* Two dots in the final barline takes you back to the beginning of the song, section, verse, or previous repeat.

Morning — Greig 1843-1907 — track 6

Joy To The World — Handel 1685-1759 — track 7

Play **dynamic contrasts**, such as *f*, *p*, *mf*, *mp* with the pan flute

🎵 Play forte by "angle out" and blowing more forcefully.

Moving the 'angle in or out' keeps the pitch steady as you blow gentler or more forcefully.

🎵 Play piano by 'angle in,' blowing gentler.

Joy Of Friendship — Beethoven — track 8

Exercise Three: *Skipping*

Skip 'every other pipe' to hear *major and minor 3rd intervals*

track 9

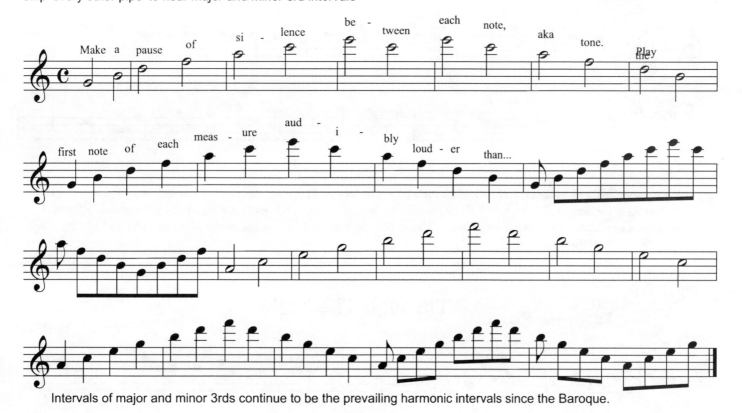

Intervals of major and minor 3rds continue to be the prevailing harmonic intervals since the Baroque.

Ear Training

Close your eyes, play any pipe, and play another. Name the tones you played, and determine the interval between them.
You can 'mark' the pipes you play with a thumb or fingers from either or both of your hands to see what you played.

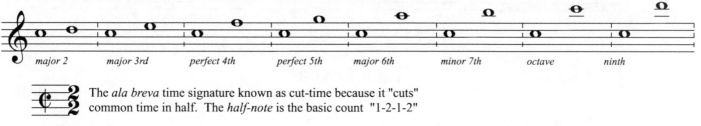

| major 2 | major 3rd | perfect 4th | perfect 5th | major 6th | minor 7th | octave | ninth |

The *ala breva* time signature known as cut-time because it "cuts"
common time in half. The *half-note* is the basic count "1-2-1-2"

Common time
abbreviated and literal

Kum Ba Ya

track 10

Nigeria

Humming Song

track 11

Schumann 1810-1856

Add *flute singing* for more tone color: • Hum into the pipe as you blow. Likely, your first singing tone will be in unison with each pipe. To sing in harmony: • Select a tune that you can play easily, • Add a bass line tone that you can sing per measure, • Practice singing the tone (a chromatic tuner, tuning forks, or a keyboard can help) • Alto or sopranos can sing 3rds, 4ths, and 5ths over the melody for sweet effects.

All Through The Night

track 12

Wales

Gary Owen

track 13

Irish Jig

The Jasmine Flower

track 14

China

Swing Low, Sweet Chariot

track 15

Kimi Ga Yo

track 16

Japan

11

Theme from "Surprise Symphony"

Haydn 1732-1809

track 17

The Farmer And The Crow

Sweden

track 18

Exercise Four: *Hopping*

track 19

Play one, hop beyond two pipes, play the third to hear *perfect 4th intervals:*

The *fourth* was the primary interval of Europe's *Renaissance* (14th to 17th century A.D.) melody and harmony.

Down In The Valley

Ye Banks And Braes

"O' Bonnie Doon..."

Aire Scotland

Fermata, ⌢ ⌣, wants you to play its note a bit longer and louder as if it were the first note of the measure.

Shenandoah

13

The Riddle Song

track 23

The Merry Plow Boy

track 24

Irish ballad

Paddy Whack

track 25

Irish jig

14

A' Roving

Staccato, the dot under or over a note *"Play the note for less time than normally."* A 'staccato note' wants more 'quiet time' in place of its 'lost time.' Staccato = less tone, more pause between tones.

Serenade

from "A Little Night Music"

The first measure of a song with more than one verse is often a *pick up* measure. Its beats added
to the beats of the final measure equal one full measure as set by the time signature.

Simple Gifts

track 28

Shaker hymn

God Rest Ye Merry Gentlemen

track 29

Exercise Five: *Jumping*

track 30

Play one pipe, jump up three pipes, play the fourth to hear *perfect fifth intervals:*

The *fifth* is the primary music interval from the classical Greek through the Medieval. The fifth and octave define the scale.

O Christmas Tree

track 31

Harvest Home

Irish hornpipe

track 32

Scherzo *(Joke)*

track 33

1. A fast, dynamic movement 2. A humorous instrumental solo

Clementi 1752-1832

Beethoven replaced the classical minuet dance movement with the scherzo as the final movement in his major compositions

Polovetsian Dances

track 34

Borodin 1818-1893

Mãruntel

track 35

Romanian dance step

Wayfaring Stranger

track 36

Religious ballad

Baidin Fheidhilmid

Irish ballad

Come, Ever-smiling Liberty

Handel 1685-1759

Exercise Six: *Leaping*

Play one, leap past four pipes play the fifth to hear *major 6th intervals:*

Jingle Bells

My Bonnie

Sea song

O Come, All Ye Faithful

Hush Little Baby
track 43

Wildwood Flower
track 44

Two Little Sisters
track 45

China

Song Of The Lark
track 46

Beethoven

21

Kingdom Coming

track 47

Henry Work

Exercise Seven: *Soaring*

Play one, soar o'r five pipes, play the sixth to hear *minor 7th intervals:*

track 48

Silent Night

track 49

Jesu, Joy Of Man's Desiring

J.S. Bach

Intervals: The sound distance between two tones

Perfect Consonant Intervals (sound pleasant)

vibration ratio*

unison	1:1
octave	1:2
perfect 5th	3:2
perfect 4th	4:3

The human ear senses the consonance or dissonance of intervals more acutely in harmony than in melody where the textures of intervals are more subliminal.

Dissonant (sounds 'distressed')

major 2nd	9:9
minor 2nd	16:15
major 7th	15:8
minor 7th	16:9

Imperfect Consonant

major 3rd	5:4
minor 3rd	6:5
major 6th	5:3
minor 6th	8:5

* Calculated in 'JI' (*just intonation*), the tuning with unaltered pitch through the octaves. The 'perfect consonant intervals' of JI are perceptibly discordant within chords. Bach `tempered' the scale so that the intervals are an equal distance throughout the octaves. His landmark composition in equal temperament is "The Well Tempered Clavier"

Theme From Fantasia

track 51

The Happy Farmer

Schumann

track 52

Country Dance

track 53

Mozart

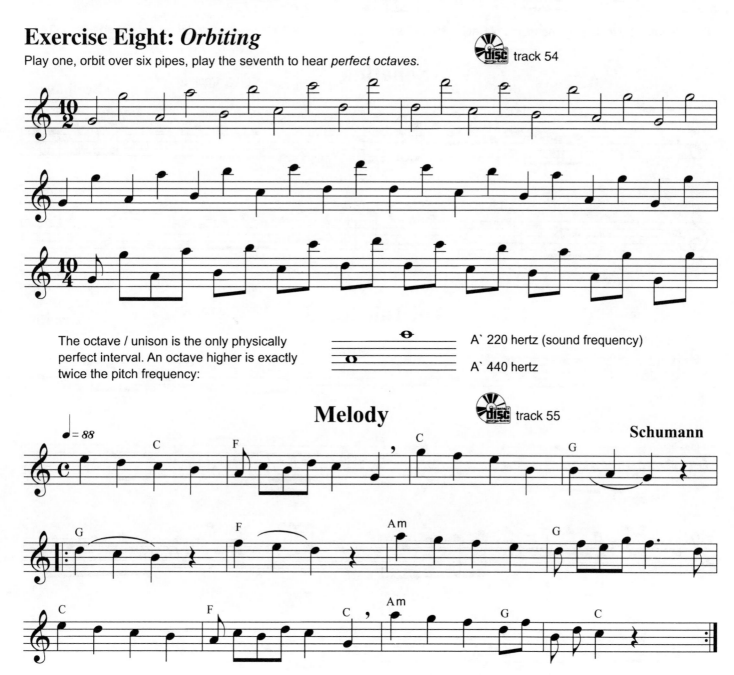

Mozart was not the only composer to "glean from the garden of folk tunes." **Schumann**, as seen on the previous page, "stalked the wild audible." **Beethoven** was such a 'farm-boy' that he earned a `vegetable nickname,' which became his last name. As you may know, he began life as 'Johan Ludwig', nonetheless, soon became 'Beet Van Hoofn' amoungst his circle of musician friends, who shaped that name into what we know today.

Exercise Eight: *Orbiting*

Play one, orbit over six pipes, play the seventh to hear *perfect octaves*.

track 54

The octave / unison is the only physically perfect interval. An octave higher is exactly twice the pitch frequency:

A` 220 hertz (sound frequency)

A` 440 hertz

Melody

track 55

Schumann

Minuet

track 56

J. S. Bach

[Please note: the final eight measures of Bach's Minuet were added after the CD was recorded, and are not on the CD.]

Sonatina

track 57

Beethoven

The Idle Road

track 58

Cronin

Hatikvah

track 59

Israel

Annie Laurie

track 60

Scots Aire

Song My Mother Taught Me

track 61

Dvořák
1841-1904

27

Exercise Nine: *C Major Harmony*

An arpeggio is the single notes of a chord played in rapid succession to suggest the chord. Practice pan flute arpeggios in a large hall, tunnel, or a ravine to add reverb. Those places will add some 'virtual sustain' to an instrument with little sustained tone.

Wind instruments excel at a different type of 'sustained tone': *long duration' sustained tones* via the players breath. The long, steady tones of winds cannot be achieved on strings or the piano. Bowed strings can make long tones, however, it comes with a distracting vibrato.

Exercise Ten: *Pentatonic (five-tone) scales*

Metronome mark: ♩ = 88
The exact tempo as set by the composer

Tempo mark: An Italian word, such as
moderato, that represents a metronome mark

Tempo marks for treble woodwinds
Adagio: slow 56 - 68
Andante: *moderato*, walking pace 72 - 96
Allegro: *brisk, lively, vivace* 102 - 168
Presto: *rapid* 172 +

Fewer tones /intervals need less harmony!

Pentatunic

Exercise Eleven: *Semi-tone higher F♯*

The sharp sign (♯) has you play `F a semi-tone higher. `F♯ sounds halfway between `F and `G.

𝄞 Hold the bottom ends of the pipes, *(feet)* out at a 45° angle as seen below

𝄞 Play the `G pipe at the 45° angle to intone F♯.

𝄞 Compare your `F♯ with `G and F to make sure that your `F♯ sounds halfway between.

𝄞 If your `F♯ is 'off', move the angle in or out.

𝄞 Additionally, you can move the angle at which you send your breath into the pipe. If you blow diagonally into the pipe the pitch will be lower, which will help to make the `G pipe sound `F♯.

Accidentals are note tones not in the key of the composition.

track 65

Angels We Have Heard On High

track 66

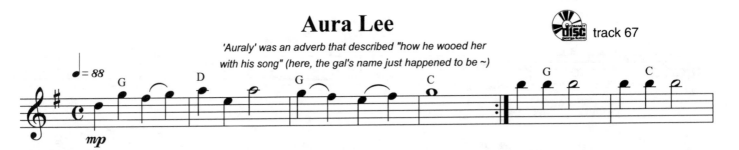

Aura Lee

track 67

'Auraly' was an adverb that described "how he wooed her with his song" (here, the gal's name just happened to be ~)

30

We Three Kings Of Orient Are

track 68

Nelly Bly

track 69

Stephen Foster

Pied Piper

track 70

Nicola Piccini 1728-1800

31

track 71   'Tis The Last Rose Of Summer

"left blooming alone..."

Irish aire

track 72   Yellow Rose Of Texas

track 73   March Of The Toys

Tchaikovsky 1840-1893

Exercise Twelve: *Semi-tone lower B♭*

The flat sign (♭) has you play `B a semi-tone lower. `B♭ sounds halfway between `B and `A.

♪ Hold the feet of the pipes out at a 40° angle as seen on page 4.

♪ Play the `A pipe at the 40° angle to intone `B♭.

♪ If your tone is not `B♭, adjust the angle at which you hold the `feet' out, and or send your breath diagonally into the pipe.

The `natural sign` ♮ ` has you bring `B♭ back to `B

Streets Of Laredo

track 75

Deck The Hall

track 76

Wales

"Deck The Hall" began as a sailor's work song titled, **"Haul The Deck"** One keen sailor inverted the title, and made a few minor changes to the lyrics for the 'haulidays. 'Haul', for example, was also an old Welsh sailor's jargon meaning "sweep." Of course, the "sweeps" link to the haulidays was well known early on. Later, the tune morphed into a pirate's song, **"Deck The Haul."** Finally, it returned as a legitimate sailor's tune, **"Hall The Deck,"** a tune sung whilst preparing for shipside concerts.

The history of tunes is often funny in a surprising way. 'Connect the dots,' though, and it will make sense.

O Katy O'Neil

Edward Rupert

track 80

New note tone: C♯ → 30° angle out on the `D² pipe

Quiz What's the dif' between 'note' and 'tone'?
Answer: The letters are re-arranged.

Theme - Sonata

Corelli 1653-1713

track 81

Senka Tankana

Peru

A *slur* is a tie (page 9) that "bridges" two or more notes tones as one continuous tone. Long slur interval demand that you move to the next pipe quickly without pause. Legato is the 'text version' of the 'slur line' for long passages of slurred tones.

The Miller's Flowers

Schubert 1797-1828

Push a pipe up 1/4" or so to 'mark your way' as you learn a passage.

Place your thumb or index on the back of pipe to help you find the pipe as you play.

Las Mañanitas

track 84

Mexico

The Little Sandman's Song

track 85

Brahms 1833-1897

Symphony # 1
First movement theme

Ode Triumphant

Brahms

track 86

Carolan's Receipt

track 87

O'Carolan 1670-1738

Mazurka

national dance step of Poland

track 88

Chopin 1810-1849

Threshold of Feeling (ouch) 130 dB

fff 90   *ff* 80   *f* 70   *mf* 60   *mp* 55   *p* 50   *pp* 40   *ppp* 30

Threshold of hearing (huh?) 0-5

Human speech

Love Is Teasin'

Irish ballad

Shule Aroon

track 90

Irish Aire

Song Dance Forms

Aire: (pronounced 'irer' even if you are not a Scot) It is a popular national melody with several poets writing song lyrics to the one melody; often in moderate, 4/4 time. The poet, Thomas Moore wrote *'Tis The Last Rose Of Summer* to the melody of an auld Irish aire, and you can find other titles of song poems that use the same aire / melody.

Ballad: Originally, a short, simple vocal melody intended for dance accompaniment, hence the air of such a song. Contemporary ballads include narrative epic lyrical poem songs, songs for single instruments in various tempi and meter.

Jig: Usually in a brisk tempo of triple or compound meter often 6/8, so that the dance movements are quite numerous and intricate. In the *Suite* form, a final, lively movement might be a gigue, the "serious" jig.

Reel: *Lively* tempo, often in *cut time* with two *reprises* (repeats) of eight measures; danced by two couples; Likely of Celtic origin as are all these dances.

Hornpipe: Old English origin in 3/2 time, now usually in 4/4 with dotted 8th tones followed by 16ths; very popular in the 18th century. Henry Purcell renewed the form in the previous century.

The Ould Orange Flute

track 91

Irish Aire

Rhythm Technique — Note tempo (in 4/4 time)__ Count and speak as you tap the rhythm

Quarter notes ♩ count *"one, two, three, four, one...*(Use "clock time" or your heart beat as the 'time-plate.')

8th notes ♪ count *"one - and, two - and, three - and, four - and, - one - and, ..."*

16th notes ♬ *"one - e - and, two - e - and, three - e - and, four - e - and,..."*

32nd notes ♬ *"one - e - uh - and, two - e - uh - and, three - e - uh - and, four - e - uh - and, ..."*

Repeat Phrases

D.C al Coda: "play from the beginning to the coda" ➙ ⊕ or the "coda re-direct" ➙ **to Coda**

D.S. al Coda: "go to the sign ➙ ℅ play to the coda" ➙ ⊕ or the "coda re-direct" ➙ **to Coda**

∽ repeat the measure once. *"5"* repeat the measure five times

Expressions

↜ **tr:** trill play two tones (often a semi-tone interval) in rapid 'back and forth' alternation

8va: play an octave higher than written

Fermata ⌒ or ⌣ play the tone louder, longer:

Tenuto – [dash-line over/under a note] play note longer, but with the same accent / loudness

Comma ' Pause for breath / dramatic effect:

Staccato: [dot under/over note] play the note shorter, more pause between tones

Legato: play the series of tones without pause between tones

rit. steadily slower, same as **rall.**